on a POWER TRIP

AFFIRMATIONS AND ACTIONS TOWARDS YOUR HIGHER-SELF

W. M. JACEY

on a POWER TRIP

AFFIRMATIONS AND ACTIONS TOWARDS YOUR HIGHER-SELF

W. M. JACEY

Copyright © 2017 All rights reserved.

Published by Wrote Goat Publishing, P.O. Box 2463, Riverside CA 92516
Printed in the USA
All Scripture quotations are taken from King James Version (KJV) of the Holy Bible.

Disclaimer statement of warranty / Limit of liability:
No part of this book may be reproduced or transmitted in any form or by any means, electronic or mechanical, including photocopying, recording or by any information storage and retrieval system, without written permission from the author or publisher. Please direct your inquiries to letstalk@wrotegoat.com. The information provided within this book is for general informational purposes only. While we try to keep the information up-to-date and correct, there are no representations or warranties, expressed or implied, about the completeness, accuracy, reliability, suitability or availability with respect to the information, products, services, or related graphics contained in this book for any purpose. Any use of this information is at your own risk. The methods describe within this book are the author's personal thoughts. They are not intended to be a definitive set of instructions for this project. You may discover there are other methods and materials to accomplish the same end result. This book contains information that is intended to help the readers be better informed consumers of affirmations as cognitive behavioral techniques of positive thinking. It is presented as general advice on positive thinking towards a higher-self. Always consult your doctor for your individual needs in health care. Before beginning any new food program or exercise program, it is recommended that you seek medical advice from your personal physician. This book is not intended to be a substitute for the medical advice of a licensed physician. The reader should consult with their doctor in any matters relating to his/her mental or physical health. The information contained within this book is strictly for educational purposes. If you wish to apply ideas contained in this book, you are taking full responsibility for your actions. The author has made every effort to ensure the accuracy of the information within this book was correct at time of publication. The author does not assume and hereby disclaims any liability to any party for any loss, damage, or disruption caused by errors or omissions, whether such errors or omissions result from accident, negligence, or any other cause.
ISBN: 978-0-692-95266-5
Library of Congress Control Number: 2017917675
Cover Illustration Copyright © 2017 For The Courageous LLC
Cover design by W. M. JACEY

CONTENTS

Imagine..1
Three Pilots and the Plane...3

SECTION ONE

AFFIRMATIONS:
the POWER and the PRACTICE

Affirmation..12
How to Affirm 13
How to Make Your Own 14
My Formula for a Successful and Powerful Affirmation 15
Back the Affirmation With Immediate Action................17
Maintenance of Your New Habit..................................18
Retiring With Gratitude..18
Prepare to Wake Up Powerful....................................18

SECTION TWO

AFFIRMATIONS and ACTIONS
TOWARDS YOUR HIGHER-SELF

Instructions..21
Anger..22
Attitude...24
Belief..26
Bitter..28
Confidence...30
Courage...32
Co-Workers / Peers...34
Depression..36
Depression in Others............*See Sickness in Others and Understanding*
Discouragement......................*See Hope, Faith and Goals*
Eating..38
Exercise...40
Faith...42
Family...44
Fear..46

Forgiveness..48
Friendship...50
Goals..52
Gratitude..54
Habit..56
Happiness...58
Hate...60
Health in Body..62
Health in Mind...64
Health in Spirit...66
Help...68
Hope..70
Jealousy..72
Loss - Death 74
Loss - Separation..76
Love...78
Mistakes...80
Money..82
Motivation...84
Occupation..86
Perfectionism...88
Regret..90
School..92
Self-Esteem..94
Self-Improvement...96
Sickness in Others..98
Sickness in You...100
Stress..102
Success ....*See Winning*
Time...104
Understanding...106
Winning..108
You..110
Dedication..112
Future Publications..113
Contact Information...114

For My Tribe

Carlotta - Chan'nel - Jaime - Edna

Imagine

What would the world be like today if productive strategies, inventions, books and all other aspirational ideas of mankind had come into fruition? What if everyone were less likely to trip over stumbling blocks, some of which they've placed in their own way, achieved their goals, thusly becoming more successful contributors to our society. And, in doing so had become a beacon for others to follow in building their own dreams.

Thank you for making the choice to continue your quest in achieving greatness. There are millions of significant self-development and coaching media out there. I suspect that this is not your first book on life-stimulating material, nor should it be your last. My hope is that this book will serve you in your journey towards your higher-self. By design, *On a Power Trip, Affirmations and Actions Towards Your Higher-Self*, will assist you with creating a healthier dialect within you through affirmations and declarations backed with specific actions.

THREE PILOTS AND THE PLANE

Three Pilots and the Plane

Do you have a goal or burning desire that you want to see come into fruition? Do you wish to be more successful than you are today; for your life to finally get off the ground and take flight? To be happy by your rules and by your design. My guess is yes…yes you do.

For this story exercise, think of your aspirations as flights and the plane is your whole being in its entirety. Your subconscious mind serves as the co-pilot and there is a cruise control button named Auto, short for auto-pilot. You are the pilot, the conscious mind who holds the final decisions.

Imagine you, the pilot, and your plane are both fired up and ready to go. You're on the runway, you are excited, the engine is roaring and your adrenalin is pumping. Other pilots in their planes behind you are watching and waiting to take their turn, wishing you a safe and fun flight. But what happens? Your co-pilot, the sub-conscious mind, starts telling you, "This isn't going to work; we shouldn't fly today because…," followed by all sorts of reasons, just and petty, that it can grab.

Your co-pilot begins to create multiple excuses and thoughts about why you should not fly today. "It's too hot or the engine might fail, it's too cold or there may be a storm, the plane is too old or it's too new." The *"because"* becomes this monstrous screaming maniac your subconscious mind releases, that is running laps around your brain over and over again. Every image of disaster your co-pilot imagines is a new head that sprouts up on the monster until it becomes so big and scary your spirit is crushed and you feel you can't possibly move forward. The anxiety your experiencing is palpable. Therefore, as the pilot you say, "Your right, I can't fly...what was I thinking." So, you drive off the runway, back into your hanger, turning your engine off; parked and paralyzed. You, all your passengers, and all the spectators, are disappointed.

What is happening?

Understand that when you say you can't fly, that it is *your conscious and final decision* as the pilot, the one in charge. Your co-pilot only produced fear based suggestions on why you shouldn't, not that you can't. As the pilot, you have the power of choice, either way. Therefore, you are responsible.

Let's continue the story. Now that it has presumably protected you, your co-pilot is feeling proud of a job well executed, and puts the multi-headed monster back into its cage. You look up and see all the other planes that were behind you take off towards their goals and dream-destinations. You notice that the other pilots take a glance of pity on you right before they lift off the ground. You are embarrassed and you feel like a failure. You can only envy how glorious it must feel to be up there, free; at which time, your co-pilot says with the loving tone, "You're not a failure, your smarter, and it's safer on land. Can't you see those other pilots are more experienced, and that they have better planes than we do? I just showed you what could happen if we flew today. Maybe we'll try again when you have more knowledge, or we get a different plane. Anyway, if God wanted you to fly he would have given you wings, right?"

Don't fire your co-pilot

Understand that since the day you were born your co-pilot was pre-programmed to defend you in a certain manner, albeit at an elementary level, and as a basic instinct. Your co-pilot is working in overdrive, pulling up scary images, while backing those up with painful memories to protect you from what it fears will hurt you if you choose to move forward. I like to call those fun little clips, *"remember when."* And whatever old images of hurt and pain are playing in your head, they bring painful emotions. In this case fear, doubt, defeat, self-loathing, pity and overall bad stress that your entire body suffers. It feels as if every image your co-pilot shows you is real today, happening right this moment, and is the absolute truth, killing your will to move forward.

As you continue to live, your co-pilot continues to learn what can physically or emotionally hurt you. This is a good thing only if you use it as an aid in making smarter decisions, but not as an excuse to fail at life by refusing to try. For example, with possible physical harm, your co-pilot stops you from placing your hand over fire, which is appropriate. Since it knows fire burns; it allows you to consider your actions before taking them, to either put on a fire-retardant glove or abandon the idea all together, depending on the reason for your *"why."* The point is, the fear is not supposed to stop you. It is there for you to take a short pause, then make the best decisions moving forward for your health, growth and character.

If there appears to be physical danger by acting on your goal, your co-pilot will attempt to protect you. Let's think of high-risk activities which can cause you physical harm or death; such as, sky diving, being a reporter in a war zone, or taking a selfie with an untamed lion for a film you are producing. Your co-pilot will immediately tell you why you shouldn't proceed in its interest of helping you to preserve your life and the life of others. For example, what if the parachute fails, what if a bomb drops, or what if you get mauled. However, if you take that basic information and understand the risk, then assure your co-pilot that you are prepared and possess the courage to face the risks to reach your *why*, then all you must do is execute your plan with action and stay the course. This is how you tame the monster your co-pilot lets loose.

Fear is not only generated for immediate physical harm; there are sneakier and greater menacing fears that manifests within us; social and emotional. For this example of fear, think of something emotionally risky that can compromise your ego such as writing a memoir, pursuing an acting career, or becoming an entrepreneur. Your co-pilot can say, "You will face ridicule if you pursue this goal. People will say, you aren't good enough, good looking enough, or smart enough. You will never succeed."

This type of dialog your co-pilot produces constructs the fear, which is the *"monster"* that stops you from moving forward and pursuing your goals and dreams. Your co-pilot is amazing and has undoubtedly saved you numerous times from real danger, but now your co-pilot has become a stick in the mud. You are mentally as well as physically exhausted and too scared to go out and live boldly. Too afraid of making mistakes and settling for merely existing in your comfort zone.

How many times has this experience happened to you?

Here is the good news, it's only temporary defeat. You have the power to change the conversation and outcome immediately – and win.

Re-train yourself and your co-pilot

In order to help your co-pilot help you, you have to first see its point of view. Second, assure and affirm the expectations you have; third, face the fears with swift action; and lastly, stay the course without fail.

Help your co-pilot understand that you appreciate and will consider its input. And, you are the *Pilot* for a reason. Give it updated information to justify your reasons for moving forward as planned through competent preparation. From there on, affirm and declare the success you foresee. And most importantly – take action! Simple, but not easy as you must change yourself first, then have the will power to lead your co-pilots as planned without waiver.

The work ahead requires building the habit of consciously and consistently fighting back negativity. This is accomplished by flooding your mind with supportive images and declaring your success. Then immediately, backing those positive thoughts with action. Regardless of how big or small the steps, any step forward becomes progressive.

You and your co-pilot will inherently learn new problem-solving information instead of placing reliance on stored apprehensions. Remember, you are the pilot. You know what you want, what's best and what path to take. You can see what's real and what is not, and you have the final say. That is where your power lies.

Gear up

The power of positive thinking is tantamount to affirming and declaring the outcome you desire. Inspiration from leadership, gratitude, faith and prayer helps you believe in what you are declaring. And to solidify the change, you must act and stick with execution of your plans.

With thousands of noes growing up and possibly people overprotecting you, alongside millions of negative images and thoughts surrounding you, you need to use reprogramming armor to block out the nay and naysayers. Armor of choice would be positive statements in the form of affirmations and declarations. This is the power of yes. Yes, you are capable. Yes, you are worthy. Yes, you can. Yes, you will. Yes, you must make this flight happen today!

Used correctly and daily, this book will assist you in creating a more constructive, progressive and loving relationship with all the little voices that make you, you. And you will attract others to share in the happiness.

Take off!

Now that you stand in your power, you rev up your engine with the positive imagery of a successful flight, knowing that you are equipped and brave enough to handle whatever lies ahead. With your co-pilots blessing, you take to the runway, heart pumping so loud you can hear it over the engine. Then…you lift off. All the other planes watching are proud of you for taking this step forward.

A few minutes later your plane is coasting and the view is spectacular. You take this moment to breathe it all in. It's everything you have dreamed of and more.

Now that you have conquered this flight, you can bring in the third pilot, Auto, to keep your plane on course. This way you and your co-pilot can focus on a new flight; a bigger dream, a new destination for the future. You're thinking of growing into a bigger and faster plane where you can bring loved ones with you. You and your co-pilot check on Auto every now and again to make sure you're all still headed in right direction, together. This my friends, is living your higher-purpose and your higher-self.

Enjoy your flight!

A Moment with the Author

"If God wanted us to fly, He would have given us wings."
– Kitty Burns

May I suggest, he skipped the wings on purpose. And thankfully. Could you imagine trying to keep 7ft wings clean every day? Or sitting down on a couch? Awkward, wouldn't you agree?

What God gave us is far more superior. The power of choice. The power to think and create wings, if we choose to, so we did. He gave us inspiration and guidelines to follow from his other creatures, called birds. I don't think it's an accident that He put these creatures in the sky. I believe God gave us a reason to look up, to remind us that He is there and *got our backs*. I know every time I look up to the sky, I feel a sense of peace and hope. The sky reminds me there are no limits, just God cheering me on. So, I breathe. Breathe in just enough hope to muster up my courage to take another step forward.

And if I happen to see a plane zooming by, I'm also reminded of how amazing we are and what we can accomplish when we put our minds together.

I don't envy the birds. They are beautiful and can take flight, but, their abilities are limited. They can't physically carry any other bird on their back while in flight. But we can.

I believe God wants you to grow, and as you continue to grow, your one-seater starter plane continues to get bigger, and bigger with cool upgrades. So big that when others need a lift you have the capacity to let them soar with you. To let them see and feel hope like you do. With your passengers' full attention, you take that opportunity to help them see what they can also have and become. And they are inspired; so inspired, they too grow and do the same for others. And it all starts right now with you. You become part of the hope. You become part of God's plan.

Believe in yourself, you are worthy – *W. M. Jacey*

SECTION ONE

AFFIRMATIONS
the POWER and the Practice

Affirmation:
To state positively, confirm and declare. An announcement of what the present state is and will be.

At the beginning stages of changing a negative conversation you are having with yourself, to the state of a positive one, the process must be simple. By design, affirmations and declarations for self-development are simple to understand, uplifting, supportive and empowers you towards your goals. Because of their simplicity, they are effective, and should not to be undervalued.

You may have heard some in leadership or coaching positions downplay this activity in order to sound enlightened. I have witnessed these occurrences many times. These individuals may say affirmations are ineffective mumbo jumbo; they are either ignoring, or not realizing the fact that they too use affirmations. Any declaration you make that states you have changed, will change, or obtain something in the future is, by default, an affirmation. And positive statements towards a fruitful outcome is the epitome for success. Therefore, lets you and I agree that affirmations are one of the most effective tools to effect the change in your pattern of thinking and, possibly your life.

Affirmations embody what you want to feel, be or have; such as a happier attitude, a healthier body weight, entering a higher income bracket, or becoming the biggest bully. Regardless, if your goal is for good or for bad, affirmations are formed from your personal wants and desires.

In regard to human nature, we know all too well that people can want things that are not good or harmonic to the community, and yet they can affirm and feel *"positive"* that they will have or accomplish it regardless of who they hurt. Understanding that this tool can be wielded either way is imperative to how you use it. The focus set forth in this book, in the use of affirmations and declarations, are for personal-growth, goal execution, dream-catching, self-love, respect and upstanding character building with the intent to do no harm.

Your affirmations should do three things: evoke emotions, reassure your higher-self, and confirm that you will remain in this state while moving forward towards your goals and dreams. Simultaneously, they give your mind a direct order to decide which road to take to obtain what you want. Since the tone is in forward motion, affirmations work because the future holds hope. Your mind embraces hope since it is trained, at the earliest age, to believe in your future which is a tremendous benefit.

How to affirm

A key to finding success in this practice is repetition. Affirm plenty, and you will begin to have expectations for the future. Declare enough, and you will truly begin to embody what you state that you are and what you will have. Creating this new positive habit will train your mind and spirit to look at the glass as not just half full, but refillable and shatter proof. You can see results immediately from some of your declarations while others may take a little time. Either way, the power lies with repetition and the continuation of developing this habit.

You should think of affirming exercises as your job. It is a vital part of transforming your life. You are the owner and the staff of the business called *"You."* And for this business to succeed and flourish, you must show up to work every day. A great practice to gain momentum and success is by doing your job three times a day; morning, afternoon and evening. In doing so, you will have created a new habit and will automatically begin to think progressively without making a conscious effort.

In the beginning of this new practice, it may feel silly or counterintuitive; but isn't the risk of feeling silly to live as your higher-self nonexistent compared to the rewards? The great news is, this practice will become habitual within sixty to ninety days. Ninety days of training is a blink-of-an-eye in perspective to a full lifetime.

How to make your own

When developing affirmations and declarations, you may find it is easier to think of them as an oath you are making, to and about yourself currently, to alter your future. These statements typically start out with I…, "I make, I see, I am," etc. Your declarations can be so strong that you feel it is not only an oath, but that *"It is done!"*

Again, you may find certain declarations a challenge when used for the first time; your mind may argue that what you are stating is a lie. For instance, if you are feeling grumpy and you declare, "I am happy!" – without hesitation, your mind rebels with, "No, I'm not." A way to overcome this is by having the mindset that your grumpiness is a thing of the past as of the second your declaration rolls off your tongue.

The affirmations in this book are simple and powerful. However, it can never be a one size fits all. For full embracement of your daily habit in affirming and declaring, I encourage you to write your own. You can start by changing one or two affirmations from each title within this book and then tailor them to your specific needs.

Example:

EXERCISE affirmation: I will exercise today.
Your created affirmation: I will complete 20 pushups today.

What I have provided you is a base, a launching pad; the ground rules for success for many areas of your life. And as you grow within your personal power, expect your affirmations and declarations to evolve as a reflection of your growth. They should become stronger and bolder to the point of specific audacity!

My formula for a successful and powerful affirmation:

1. Less is more.
Affirmations and declarations are stronger when direct. This means, fewer words to get the point across. Thus, piercing your spirit faster.

Example:

Too wordy: I will exercise today and complete 20 pushups during my workout.
Precise: I will complete 20 pushups today.

It is okay to have lengthy sentences if it is something super specific you are looking to attain. You can even put sentences together from different objectives to create one cohesive intent. It all depends on your goal. Just keep it as clean as possible so your mind does not have to over process and/or deviate from the desired goal.

2. Affirmation tonality.
It is commonly said, "You get what you ask for from the universe." In many cases I have seen people create their affirmations and declarations with negative tonalities simply because they were not taught any better. To avoid this

mistake, be sure to keep the words positive in the sentences you create. Avoid words such as no, not, can't, won't, bad, worst, hate, etcetera. This may take a little practice. Let's use an example of a great day.

Example 1:

Weak tonality: I won't have a bad day today.
Powerful tonality: I will make this a great day!

There is no need to remind yourself of a *bad* day.

Example 2:

Weak tonality: I will not get fired today.
Powerful tonality: I am an asset to the team! *Or,* I will keep my job.

Example 3:

Weak and negative tonality: No one will bother me today.
Powerful and positive tonality: Everyone respects my time.

Important Note:

The *only* exception to the use of negative words, or bad grammar in your affirmations, statements or declarations, is when using a popular phrase for fun. I have provided a few in this literature under 'Fun Affirmation' and 'Fun Statement'. For example, *"Let's get it on like Donkey Kong,"* can be used for stirring up courage. We have all heard these types of sayings at one point or another. You find them in music, television, books and social media. These sayings go viral because they're typically riddled with bad grammar, or they are naughty or phrased with huge ego, therefore, making them so much fun to employ. These popular sayings tend to lighten the mood. They empower the user and help to break the negativity. So have fun, lighten up, and feel free to use them in your practice.

Back the affirmation with immediate action

To change your circumstances, a bold statement such as an affirmation, backed with immediate action, are the steps you want to take in achieving your goal. The moment you declare, "I *am* happy," physically move your body towards that goal by putting a smile on your face and changing your thoughts to positive imagery, and you will begin to experience change at that moment. The practice of affirming will lose its effectiveness if you neglect to physically move towards the outcome you hope for. You must do the work.

Action is the ultimate key and crucial to your success. Although you are speaking to and into yourself, possibly chanting your affirmations out loud or in your head, declaring affirmations is rarely enough. You must back it up with action!

Example:

Affirmation: I am an artist. (When in fact, you have never drawn in your life.)
Action: Immediately take out the closest piece of paper, even a gum wrapper will do. Grab a writing tool and draw!

Of course, this is a hyper-simplified example, but a real one nonetheless. How many talented people, including yourself, do you know, wish they could act on their desires, yet, do not pursue them, and never live the dream. There are only two types of people in the world. Those who do, and those who do not, and most of the time by choice. My hope is that you train yourself to be a doer.

Maintenance of your new habit

Find a few affirmations and declarations you need now, and make multiple copies and place them on your restroom mirror; your wall or nightstand of your bedroom; your pocket or purse for work and so on. You can make a digital note or wall paper of your devices as well. For quick reference, keep this book in an area you frequent. And if you live with family, they should have their own copy so yours does not disappear.

Retiring with gratitude

Though your mind continues to work while you are asleep, you can influence what it mulls over. Take five to ten minutes before retiring to count your blessings for what you have now and for what's coming. This will ensure your mind is focusing on positive imagery, helping you feel at peace. You can either recite your gratitude out loud, or jot it down on a piece of paper in silence to feel it in your spirit. As well, you can read material that focuses on gratefulness that you may have written already, or from literature you have acquired. Doing this exercise nightly will help you rest and wake with a positive spirit. If you are married or have others in the home, do this exercise together and your household will grow to become harmonic.

Prepare to wake up powerful!

Memorize the strongest affirmation or declaration that you need to overcome the challenge you are facing now and that speaks power into your higher-self. This way you can recite it by heart when you wake. Reciting bold positive declarations about yourself before you even open your eyes allows you to be at your best, even before you step out of bed. The wrong side of the bed no longer exists. So, flip through the titles and pages in this book that holds the key to unlocking your potential right away. Find the ones that speak to your heart and immediately make them your tools to success.

SECTION TWO

AFFIRMATIONS and ACTIONS Towards Your HIGHER-SELF

The following pages are a combination of over forty different goals, emotional states, reactions or physicalities you may encounter in your everyday pursuit of developing your higher-self. For effectiveness and ease of use:

Step 1) Look up a goal, emotional state, reaction or physicality that you want to have or want to change. For example, if you are angry, you can look up ANGER, HAPPINESS, PEACE and/or FORGIVENESS. Read the entire page. Then take one or two sentences to state repeatedly.

Step 2) Complete a call to action labeled *Action Steps, Mood Adjusters,* or *Courage Juice,* that is assigned to the title of that page.

Step 3) At the end of your day take a moment to reflect with gratitude. Set a goal for the following day, and memorize an affirmation to recite when you wake.

Step 4) Commit to energizing the start of your day with proper habits such as meditation, reading, exercise, and etcetera, for internal motivation and inspiration.

ANGER

Definition: When you feel annoyed, displeased or provoked to hostility.

"He that is slow to wrath is of great understanding."
Proverbs 14:29

- I am in control.
- I breathe in positivity.
- I am patient and calm.
- I possess the strength to handle this properly.
- I can grow from this.
- I respond with love.
- My power comes from love in my heart.
- I will overcome this challenge.
- I remain cool under pressure.
- This day…*is* a great one.

Fun Statement
Keep it movin'!

Mood Adjusters
Change your location. Changing your location, even for just a moment, is a pattern-interrupt that will allow you and others a cooling off period. Physically moving your body allows you to clear your mind and heightens your mood; so walk it off.

Watch something funny. It's easier than ever to grab your media device to watch something funny. It's a temporary yet effective move in the right direction to releasing negativity or anger.

Your Power Affirmations

_____

_____

_____

_____

_____

_____

_____

_____

_____

_____

_____

_____

_____

_____

_____

Become your Higher-Self

ATTITUDE

Definition: How you think, feel or behave that reflects your state of mind or disposition.

"Fulfil ye my joy, that ye be likeminded, having the same love." Philippians 2:2

- My attitude is awesome and infectious.
- I have the spirit of a warrior.
- I control my emotional roller coaster.
- I alone have the power to alter my spirit.
- I am powered by love and light.
- I only speak words of strength and power.
- I am grateful for everything I have.
- I can do anything with my can-do attitude.
- I bounce back from all challenges.
- I am a winner.

Fun Affirmation
I rock!

Mood Adjusters
Reflect on your aspirations. Close your eyes, slow your breathing, and think on your aspirations and dreams. Imagine how you behave and what role you play in these dreams. Most likely you are envisioning your higher-self. Then, open your eyes and be that person of your dreams.

Write down your mission. Create a mission statement based off your aspirations. By the time you are done with this exercise, your attitude will be at a heightened level and the current annoyances you are experiencing will seem small.

Your Power Affirmations

Become your Higher-Self

BELIEF

Definition: Your faith, trust and confidence in yourself, someone and/or something.

"We are confident, I say, and willing..."
2nd Corinthians 5:08

- I believe in the *power of me*.
- I accomplish what I work on.
- I trust that others are here to help me.
- I trust my ability to overcome obstacles.
- I have faith in God for the right results.
- There is success in my future.
- I believe in the outcome I envision.
- I have faith in my capabilities.
- I act according to my positive beliefs.
- God believes I can, therefore, I will.

Fun Statement
Watch me!

Courage Juice
Find inspiration. Watching or listening to others triumph will empower you to feel that you can win too.

Move forward with purpose. The greatest test of your belief system is to move forward while uncertain. Stepping forward is the greatest challenge you will face when confronting opposition. Create the habit of moving towards *"go"* faster.

Talk with someone. A friend who knows your fears and strengths, can offer you encouragement and guidance.

Your Power Affirmations

Become your Higher-Self

BITTER

Definition: Unpleasant feelings you have towards someone, something or an experience.

"...ye have suffered a while, make you perfect, stablish, strengthen, settle you." 1 Peter 5:10

- I am grateful.
- I will grow from this experience.
- I use trials as stepping stones to greatness.
- I entertain great energy.
- I handle life's tests with grace.
- I spend my time around positive people.
- I have bigger blessings ahead.
- I control my mood.
- My smile is the best response.
- I go to bed fulfilled.

Fun Affirmation
I stay 'woke'!

Mood Adjusters

Take out a piece of paper and write. List who or what you are grateful for until one gives you a pleasant pause. Reflect on that one person or thing for a moment. Now, breathe deeply to soak in all the good vibes until it alters your energy.

Seek. Find the lesson or create a purpose for you and others in order to grasp the set back and hurt you're feeling.

Stay busy. If you are sulking, jump into unfinished work or a hobby; or surround yourself with people you enjoy.

Your Power Affirmations

_____

_____

_____

_____

_____

_____

_____

_____

_____

_____

_____

_____

_____

_____

_____

Become your Higher-Self

CONFIDENCE

Definition: Believing in yourself, your power and capabilities.

"The rock of my strength, and my refuge, is in God."
Psalm 62:7

- I am empowered.
- I love what I see in the mirror.
- I speak with certainty.
- My attire portrays strength.
- I create room for growth.
- I listen to music that pumps up my ego.
- I have clear goals and boldly move forward.
- I have inner peace because I am honest.
- I build trust with others by keeping my commitments.
- I am strong under pressure.

Fun Affirmation
I am da' bomb.com!

Courage Juice
Posture perfect. Erect your posture from head to toe immediately. Studies suggest this gives you a boost in testosterone. This chemical change promotes feelings of power.

Live morally and ethically. Being anything else but honest and reliable is a weakness that erodes inner strength.

Flawless. Looking your best at all times while also focusing on great posture is easy to implement. Such powerful habits are imperative for living with constant confidence.

Your Power Affirmations

Become your Higher-Self

COURAGE

Definition: Your ability to face difficulty.

"...be strong in the Lord, and in the power of His might." Ephesians 6:10

- Today I show and prove.
- I am capable.
- My higher-self is in control.
- I am moving forward.
- I stand up for myself and my beliefs.
- I have the courage to change.
- I have the courage to speak up.
- I can do all things through Christ.
- I overcome my challenges by taking action.
- I am equipped with everything I need to win.

Fun Statement
It's go time!

Courage Juice
Read John 15. You will realize you are not alone after reassurance from the written word in this passage.

Remember, you are still alive and filled with a purpose. God has not cut you off, therefore you have backup.

Pump up the music, and sing out loud to feel powerful!

Do what scares you. Complete the task you are most afraid of facing at the beginning of your day. This is crucial in setting the right tone for your day. You will have proven your courage and eliminated built up anxiety.

Your Power Affirmations

Become your Higher-Self

CO-WORKERS / PEERS

Definition: A person engaged in a similar position in your profession.

"Though war should rise against me, in this I will be confident." Psalm 27:3

- Today I prove.
- I give my peak performance under pressure.
- I am *the* key player.
- I've achieved my position because I am capable.
- I serve to please God and my goals.
- I am brave around my teammates.
- My colleagues respect me.
- I am responsible for my own actions.
- My work ethic and results are stellar.
- I am equipped with everything I need to win.

Fun Affirmation
I will rise to the top!

Action Steps

Look past today. Keep your career goals in the forefront. Never let your guard down and always behave as if you own the company.

Consciously, start and end your work day strong.

Deliberately and consistently groom better than everyone. Learn the position you aspire to attain. Listen to water cooler talk but don't engage (know thy enemy). Always give your best while you are there. Know who to know, to move ahead.

Your Power Affirmations

Become your Higher-Self

DEPRESSION

Definition: A sadness or hopelessness within you.

"The Lord also will be a refuge for the oppressed, a refuge in times of trouble." Psalm 9:9

- Today I will live.
- I possess the willpower to get up.
- I love myself enough to fight this feeling.
- I am more powerful than this emotion.
- I am loved by God and I trust in him for healing.
- I appreciate everything I have and everyone I know.
- I am grateful for my life and will live it celebrating.
- I will keep moving forward.
- I see hope in every situation.
- I can lead myself to a happy place.

Empowered Affirmation
This is my battle to win!

Courage Juice
Prayer of gratitude. Take time right now to count your blessings. Think of someone or a memory that brings you joy and inner peace.

Professional help. If needed, obtain help as soon as possible to receive healing; albeit a chemical imbalance or a situational circumstance, you deserve to live a full life.

Tell friends and family. Opening up to those you can confide in allows you to replace oppressive negativity with positive feelings of love and support. Battles are not always won alone.

Your Power Affirmations

Become your Higher-Self

EATING

Definition: The food or other items you ingest into your body.

"Whether therefore ye eat, or drink, or whatsoever ye do, do all to the glory of God." 1 Corinthians 10:31

- I make great food choices.
- I forgive myself for past behaviors.
- Eating right tastes like winning.
- My meals are balanced.
- I have crazy-ninja skills in the kitchen.
- I eat to serve my body.
- Healthy body, healthy life.
- My choices strengthen my body.
- Counting calories is a game I win.
- I have a great relationship with food.

Fun Affirmation
I persist to resist!

Action Steps
Seek assistance. Find a nutritionist or speak to your medical physician to help you with your goals. No two people are the same, so be wary of specific diet plans pushed in main stream media.

One small change. Eliminate one junk food item from your eating regimen. Replace it with one healthy food item that gives you the same result in satisfaction. Once it becomes a staple, move on to the next item and repeat the same process.

Your Power Affirmations

_____

_____

_____

_____

_____

_____

_____

_____

_____

_____

_____

_____

_____

_____

_____

Become your Higher-Self

EXERCISE

Definition: Activities you perform to sustain or improve your health and body.

"...your body is the temple of the Holy Ghost which is in you, which ye have of God." 1 Corinthians 6:19

- I can and I will push myself.
- I will get up and work my body.
- I will achieve *my* ultimate body goals.
- My healthy body is the key to my success.
- I forgive myself for past behaviors.
- I move faster.
- I am disciplined for delayed gratification.
- Exercising is sexy.
- I am more powerful than yesterday.
- I love the burn.

Fun Affirmation
Willpower is my name, killing-it is my game!

Action Steps

Pre-plan. Take out your workout clothes hours before your workout to serve as a reminder and as motivation. For example, if you want to work out right after you wake up, take out your exercise clothes the night before.

Start anywhere. Begin with stretches at home or at work as a step towards building your healthy habits in exercising.

No short cuts. Have patience with yourself and your *'body goals'*. Shortcuts will likely come with short-comings and setbacks.

Your Power Affirmations

Become your Higher-Self

FAITH

Definition: Your unshakable belief in something when there is no proof in any particular outcome. Belief that God is there.

"Now faith is the substance of things hoped for, the evidence of things not seen." Hebrews 11:1

- I possess an unbreakable faith.
- My success is the result of faith and action.
- My belief system grows stronger every day.
- I trust in God for the right outcome.
- I am capable.
- God puts challenges in front of me for a reason.
- I have hope.
- I have an unshakable trust to go after my dreams.
- I walk by faith, not by sight.
- I am an obstacle slayer.

Fun Affirmation
Victory is mine!

Courage Juice
Read Mark 11:24. Read and connect to this passage in order to find strength and courage.

Move on. If you control the outcome, move forward without hesitation. If the outcome is out of your control, hand it to God and move on with your day, not dwelling in fear.

Remember. Do not be tied to any outcome. Some are to win, some are to learn, some are to strengthen.

Your Power Affirmations

Become your Higher-Self

FAMILY

Definition: Descendants from your common ancestor or a group living together.

"He that troubleth His own house shall inherit the wind." Proverbs 11:29

- My family deserves *my* best.
- I control my actions around loved ones.
- I apologize when wrong.
- I forgive automatically.
- I protect my family in all ways I can control.
- I am a role model and inspiration to my family.
- I am worthy of respect from all family members.
- I say I love you every day to those in my home.
- I am thankful for family that also act as friends.
- I love my family unconditionally.

Fun Affirmation
We pray together and stay together!

Action Steps
Who needs a phone call today? If you are thinking of them then they are also thinking of you. Close the bridge of non-communication and call them.

Plan an outing. Money is not an excuse to skip out on fun and quality time with family. The fond memories you create strengthens the bond.

Give a hug and say, "I Love You." No time like the present to physically connect to those you care about.

Your Power Affirmations

Become your Higher-Self

FEAR

Definition: The emotion you feel when you believe something is a threat or going to inflict pain.

"He shall cover thee with His feathers, and under His wings shalt thou trust." Psalm 91:04

- Today I live in peace.
- God is my shield and my sword.
- I display courage and act with certainty.
- I am brave and accept my challenges.
- I am fluid and stepping into my destiny.
- I expect the best results.
- I am stronger than any situation.
- I am my own super hero.
- I find my strength working through my emotions.
- Yes I am awesome. Yes I can. Yes I will succeed!

Fun Statement
Game on!

Courage Juice
Imagine the outcome you want and physically move towards that goal. Immediately taking a small step is the *key* in overcoming your fears.

Read the entire passage of Psalm 91 for encouragement.

Study media that educates you in building self-esteem and confidence.

Call a confidant for guidance or to simply be your cheerleader.

Your Power Affirmations

_____

_____

_____

_____

_____

_____

_____

_____

_____

_____

_____

_____

_____

_____

_____

_____

_____

Become your Higher-Self

FORGIVENESS

Definition: When you stop blaming or feeling resentment towards someone, something or an event.

"For if ye forgive men their trespasses, your heavenly Father will also forgive you." Matthew 6:14

- I live with understanding of others.
- When I forgive others, it sets me free.
- I forgive to grant myself peace.
- I live with love in my heart.
- My mind is uncluttered because I forgive.
- I cast all my cares on God.
- God forgives me when I forgive others.
- I have been forgiven.
- I forgive myself.
- I learned a lesson and now I move on.

Fun Statement
It's all good!

Action Steps
Replace the words 'F@*k You' with 'Forgive You' every time you are provoked and you will feel the difference.

Give someone a chance to reconcile. You must communicate your grievance in order to expect an apology. And if no apology is forthcoming, find closure in knowing you have done all you can do. Then **write a letter** with your grievance and throw it away, then move on.

Boss up and apologize when you have done someone harm, even if they did not ask for one.

Your Power Affirmations

_____
_____
_____
_____
_____
_____
_____
_____
_____
_____
_____
_____
_____
_____
_____
_____

Become your Higher-Self

FRIENDSHIP

Definition: Your mutual bond outside of family or sexual relations.

"Greater love hath no man than this, that a man lay down his life for his friends." John 15:13

- I am worthy of true friendship.
- I am grateful for the friends I have.
- I grow into healthier friendships.
- I attract quality people into my circle.
- I have open communication with friends.
- I am 100% me around everyone, always.
- I am worthy of celebration.
- I have different friends for different reasons.
- My friends respect my boundaries.
- I contribute and receive in every relationship.

Fun Affirmation
We are #squadgoals!

Action Steps

Recognize why you want the friendship. This way you do not count on one person serving *all* your friendship needs, and vice versa.

Network. As you grow, so does your need for different influences around you. Do not be afraid to create new friendships.

Call. Spend quality time together. It may be best to set meet-up dates ahead of time instead of last minute notices.

Your Power Affirmations

Become your Higher-Self

GOALS

Definition: The object in which your actions are directed.

"But seek ye first the kingdom of God, and His righteousness; and all these things shall be added unto you." Matthew 6:33

- Today I am succeeding in all things.
- I alone, am responsible in seeing this goal through.
- I take my intentions seriously.
- My dreams are meant to be realized.
- My goals are set to be accomplished.
- I am courageous enough to complete my plan.
- Working on my dreams gives me strength.
- Every aspiration I have will have a resolution.
- I see myself as a success.
- I finish what I start.

Fun Statement
Winners win!

Courage Juice
Acknowledge and work within your strengths that will take you to the finish line. Leverage other people's talents to compensate where you lack in capabilities.

Take one step forward. Procrastination destroys goals.

Revisit your *why*. To find motivation when facing an uphill battle, reflect on why you want to achieve this goal.

Communicate your goal to others you trust to increase your determination towards completing your plans.

Your Power Affirmations

_____
_____
_____
_____
_____
_____
_____
_____
_____
_____
_____
_____
_____
_____
_____
_____
_____
_____

Become your Higher-Self

GRATITUDE

Definition: Your spirit of being grateful and thankful.
Willingness to show appreciation.

"In every thing give thanks."
1 Thessalonians 5:18

- I have an attitude of gratitude.
- I am thankful I am here and alive.
- I appreciate every little thing I have.
- I am blessed that *I can* face challenges.
- I express gratitude to others for their time.
- I am grateful for the love I receive.
- I graciously accept compliments.
- Thankfulness enriches my life.
- I accept gratitude from others graciously.
- I *feel* truly blessed.

Fun Statement
Blessings on blessings on blessings!

Action Steps

List. Make a list of those who have helped you. Call them personally, or email, text or send them a letter in the mail. You may go a step further and send a small token of your appreciation. Either way, do not let another moment go by without expressing your gratefulness. You will be amazed at how this action will strengthen your relationships.

Accept. Learn to accept gratitude from others – you are worthy. To turn it away will not only show your weakness or low self-esteem, but may also offend the giver.

Your Power Affirmations

_____
_____
_____
_____
_____
_____
_____
_____
_____
_____
_____
_____
_____
_____
_____
_____

Become your Higher-Self

HABIT

Definition: Your habitual behavior learned by repetition over a period of time.

"And be not conformed to this world: but be ye transformed..." Romans 12:2

- I declare happiness in my life every day.
- I make it a point to look great daily.
- Every day I celebrate who I am.
- I live my life performing at my best.
- I live my life thankful to have it.
- My exceptional habits separate me from the average.
- I eat right at every meal.
- I read daily to grow.
- I am in constant development.
- I leave my best on the table every day.

Fun Affirmation
I have wealth building habits!

Action Steps
Grab a paper and pen and draw a vertical line. On the left side write down a list of bad habits. On the right side write down items to replace those habits. Choose 1 – 2 habits to work on for 90 days until the positive action becomes your new habit.

Persistence. Patience and practice is the name of the game in acquiring a strong habit. There are no short cuts in developing strengths that become second nature.

Your Power Affirmations

_____
_____
_____
_____
_____
_____
_____
_____
_____
_____
_____
_____
_____
_____
_____
_____

Become your Higher-Self

HAPPINESS

Definition: Your feelings of joyfulness and fulfillment.

"And whoso trusteth in the Lord, happy is he."
Proverbs 16:20

- My glass is refillable.
- Happiness is my choice and my birthright.
- Every moment God grants me is a gift.
- I appreciate all that I have.
- I am blessed today and every day.
- I am happy in my journey of growth.
- I celebrate my originality.
- I light up every room.
- Helping others brings me fulfillment.
- Loving myself brings me joy.

Fun Affirmation
I dance in the rain on my parade!

Mood Adjusters
Right this second, place a smile on your face, pop your chest out, look up, tell yourself how awesome you are, breathe in deeply and hold for 5 seconds, then repeat as needed.

Find a mirror and smile at your reflection. Tell yourself how awesome you are and what a great day it will be.

Do something. Accomplish something today that is positive and gratifying, regardless of what others think.

Your Power Affirmations

_____

_____

_____

_____

_____

_____

_____

_____

_____

_____

_____

_____

_____

_____

_____

Become your Higher-Self

HATE

Definition: Intense hostility towards someone or something.

"If a man say, I love God, and hateth his brother, he is a liar." 1 John 4:20

- I act with love.
- I live to love.
- Love in, love out.
- I focus on the positives.
- Love is a far better energy.
- Love and optimism strengthens me.
- I am grateful for everything in my life at this moment.
- I apply grace and love to every challenging situation.
- People love me.
- I give great energy.

Fun Affirmation
I am not a 'hater'!

Mood Adjusters

Change your energy. Moving to a different location for a short while will help alter your attitude. You can use this time to reflect on the positives in your life.

Refer to the section on <u>Forgiveness</u>. You can begin to heal with forgiveness.

Refer to the section on <u>Gratitude</u>.

Once calm, break down the problem and identify what specifically angered you and begin to work on the solution.

Your Power Affirmations

_____
_____
_____
_____
_____
_____
_____
_____
_____
_____
_____
_____
_____
_____
_____
_____

Become your Higher-Self

HEALTH IN BODY

Definition: Your current physical state.

"...for the temple of God is holy, which temple ye are."
1 Corinthians 3:17

- I achieve a healthy weight and size.
- I appreciate my body.
- I live fit-conscious.
- I aspire to have great health insurance.
- I love every ounce of myself.
- I protect myself sexually in every occasion.
- I have a healthy relationship with food.
- I choose natural remedies if possible.
- I make the right food choices every day.
- I feel accomplished after exercising.

Fun Affirmation
I shake it off!

Action Steps

Schedule time to complete a series of light stretches. What is great, you can do them anywhere, anytime, starting now.

Target. Today, identify and target one area you want to see change in your body. Make one change in your routine today towards that goal.

Find an accountability buddy. Someone who will help keep you motivated and hold you to the fire.

Your Power Affirmations

Become your Higher-Self

HEALTH IN MIND

Definition: Your current mental state that affects your life.

"If the world hate you, ye know that it hated me before it hated you." John 15:18

- I speak greatness into my life.
- I am in control of my emotions.
- I read or listen to uplifting media throughout the day.
- I surround myself with positive people.
- I protect my energy aura from gossip.
- I look for intelligent solutions.
- A healthy body leads to a healthy mind.
- I reflect on gratefulness before sleep.
- I schedule time to reboot.
- I focus on goals and dreams when I wake.

Fun Affirmation
I am positively positive!

Mood Adjusters

Eliminate aggravations. Toxic people should be removed from your life. Disassociation can be done overnight or over time.

Forgive yourself. This is one of the biggest secrets for mental health. Forgiving *you* eliminates mental garbage that weighs your spirit down.

List and catalog your top three positive personality traits or talents. Have this list of pros on hand to call on in a moment's notice when you are feeling low, in order to feel uplifted.

Your Power Affirmations

_____

_____

_____

_____

_____

_____

_____

_____

_____

_____

_____

_____

_____

_____

_____

_____

Become your Higher-Self

HEALTH IN SPIRIT

Definition: Your current overall feelings or perspective on life.

"...according to the riches of His glory, to be strengthened with might by His Spirit in the inner man." Ephesians 3:16

- Love flows through me.
- I focus on virtues.
- God provides me with all that I need.
- All my relationships are enriched.
- I make quality time for family and friends.
- I live ethically and morally.
- I have a happy home.
- My efforts are best used on what I can control.
- I am a giver and receiver in all things good.
- God keeps me at peace.

Fun Statement
'Funday' every day!

Courage Juice

Notify everyone. Inform your boss (or yourself), your spouse, kids or any other dependents, and schedule a day or two for a time out! Work on *you* and give back to *yourself* during that time.

Daydream as a child and take time to remember what you wanted in life. Then take one step forward towards that dream.

Your Power Affirmations

_____

_____

_____

_____

_____

_____

_____

_____

_____

_____

_____

_____

_____

_____

_____

_____

Become your Higher-Self

HELP

Definition: When you give or receive assistance or support.

"The Lord shall fight for you, and ye shall hold your peace." Exodus 14:14

- I believe in teamwork.
- I am secure in myself; therefore, I ask for help.
- I am approachable to others in need.
- I offer my assistance with goodwill.
- When I succeed, they succeed.
- When they succeed, I succeed.
- Right now, moving forward makes the most sense.
- The best of us utilize other people's strengths.
- I find strength in teamwork.
- I am Gods big helper!

Fun Statement
There's no I in team!

Courage Juice
Ask. If you need help, simply ask. Only a weak minded individual is scared, egotistical and immobile. That is not you.

Receive what is owed. If you expect monetary pay, name recognition, or quid pro quo, then state your expectations upfront. This also takes courage and a strong character. Or else, you may resent the favors you give.

Accept assistance. If someone offers you a hand, show appreciation for the gesture.

Your Power Affirmations

Become your Higher-Self

HOPE

Definition: Your feelings of faith in the possibilities you want.

"Be strong and of a good courage, fear not nor, be afraid..." Deuteronomy 31:6

- God provides me with all I need to succeed.
- I am an achiever.
- I am a receiver of love today.
- My challenges are for me to conquer.
- The path I am on is God's reply to my hearts desires.
- I attract all that is great today.
- I count my blessings.
- I am working *in* my dreams and goals today.
- God gave me these wants in my heart to be realized.
- I finish what I start.

Fun Statement
Hope floats!

Courage Juice
Dream vividly. You will feel powerful after envisioning what you hope for. This is commonly achieved through meditation.

Plan on paper. Start with the end game in mind. List what needs to be done to achieve your goal. From there you will discover your first step.

Start. Today, execute an item on the list you created, then schedule a step to complete tomorrow and so forth. Do not grow weary of road blocks. Expect them.

Your Power Affirmations

Become your Higher-Self

JEALOUSY

Definition: When you feel resentment towards someone or their achievements and advantages.

"Thou shalt not covet thy neighbour's house..."
Exodus 20:17

- I love everything about myself.
- I am consumed with my own blessings.
- I have amazing features I love to flaunt.
- I focus on developing my own talents.
- I am worthy of unconditional love.
- I water my own grass.
- Watching others succeed gives me guidance.
- My success is celebrated by those who matter.
- My strengths will carry me to unparalleled success.
- I win when I work in my own strengths.

Fun Affirmation
I'm blessed for success!

Action Steps

Create a list. Make a list of qualities you love about yourself and create a game plan to strengthen and utilize those talents.

Stop. As soon as you find yourself dwelling on others, redirect your focus to a project that is entirely your own.

See section on <u>Gratitude</u>. Remember your blessings God granted you, and remember that everyone has shortcomings.

Your Power Affirmations

Become your Higher-Self

LOSS - DEATH

Definition: Your feelings of emptiness and sadness at the end of life of a loved one.

"Let not your heart be troubled, neither let it be afraid." John 14:27

- I am living today with strength.
- I am blessed for the support I have from others.
- It's okay that I grieve my own way.
- God is handling my heart and theirs.
- I move forward out of respect for those who love me.
- Healing is mine by the minute.
- I control my emotions through love and forgiveness.
- I count my blessings.
- I smile, reflecting on love.
- I move forward with more strength than yesterday.

Strength Affirmation
Through God, I am strong in this!

Courage Juice
Realize your blessings. Focus on gratitude for the memories you have of your lost loved one. And, for the family and friends you continue the journey with.

Reach out. Ask for support from others through this part of your journey in life. It should not be handled in solitude.

Find meaning. Give your energy by pouring comfort into others who are also experiencing loss.

Your Power Affirmations

_____

_____

_____

_____

_____

_____

_____

_____

_____

_____

_____

_____

_____

_____

_____

Become your Higher-Self

LOSS - SEPERATION

Definition: Your feelings of emptiness and sadness if deprived of someone or something.

"But my God shall supply all your need according to His riches in glory by Christ Jesus." Philippians 4:19

- With God, I am strong in all things.
- This situation builds my character.
- I will paint the silver lining.
- There will be a turn for the better as soon as I let go.
- I'm embracing new relationships and opportunities.
- I take the time to reflect and learn.
- I can replace this in an instant.
- My new win is around the corner.
- Fond memories are what I choose to reflect on.
- I am living this day to the fullest.

Fun Affirmation
I'm stronger and wiser!

Mood Adjusters

See sections <u>Gratitude</u> and <u>Attitude</u>.

Control. Focus on what is in front of you instead of dwelling about the past.

Realize. This loss may free you for something greater in your journey ahead. Remain open to new possibilities.

Enjoy. Reflect on the positive memories while releasing your attachment to them.

Your Power Affirmations

Become your Higher-Self

LOVE

Definition: Your strong affections for a person, place or thing.

"There is no fear in love; but perfect love casteth out fear." 1 John 4:18

- Only love makes it to heaven.
- I give and receive hugs.
- I give and receive smiles.
- I attract unconditional love.
- Love is the foundation for success in all things.
- I am secure enough to give and receive affection.
- I love myself enough to grow every day.
- I love myself enough to require respect.
- Love is for everyone.
- I am worthy of love.

Fun Statement
Love conquers all!

Courage Juice
State out loud and declare what you love about yourself.

Reach out. Contact someone today and be a good listener. Infer no judgement.

Show and tell. Do more than verbalizing your love and display your affection as well.

Love yourself enough. If a relationship is counterproductive to your happiness, take steps to dissolve the relationship.

Your Power Affirmations

_____
_____
_____
_____
_____
_____
_____
_____
_____
_____
_____
_____
_____
_____
_____
_____

Become your Higher-Self

MISTAKES

Definition: A wrong or misguided judgment or action you made.

"In whom we have redemption through His blood, even the forgiveness of sins." Colossians 1:14

- Regardless of the outcome, I take action.
- I atone with people immediately.
- I can forgive others.
- I focus and work through my challenges.
- I forgive myself.
- I possess the courage to grow from this.
- Learning is part of the game.
- Miscalculations are learning opportunities.
- I take accountability for my decisions.
- I am awesome anyway.

Fun Affirmation
Onwards and upwards!

Courage Juice
Face it. Whatever is eating at your spirit, due to a lapse in judgement, make steps towards corrections today.

Ego. Misplaced ego should never stop an apology from you. If you have offended someone, address the situation in person or over the phone. Avoid using email or text, as your intent can be misunderstood.

Forgive. Exonerate yourself for being human.

Your Power Affirmations

Become your Higher-Self

MONEY

Definition: A medium of exchange in the form of notes and coins.

"But thou shalt remember the Lord thy God: for it is He that giveth thee power to get wealth..."
Deuteronomy 8:18

- Money is a great servant.
- I proudly live within my means.
- I set limits when gaming for fun.
- I save 10% or more of every paycheck.
- Money is a tool I use to build a great life.
- I maintain great credit.
- I employ wise money habits.
- God wants me to be fruitful.
- Money flows my way.
- I pay what I owe because I can.

Fun Affirmation
I pay it forward!

Action Steps

Start a ledger. Keep track on what monies come in and go out. If there are expenses no longer serving your needs, eliminate them.

Research. Study techniques to become financially responsible, and incorporate one action item to form a new wealth building habit. Then repeat.

Reach out. Contact someone who has financial success and ask for guidance on how to incorporate the basics.

Your Power Affirmations

Become your Higher-Self

MOTIVATION

Definition: Your desire or willingness to do something.

"And whatsoever ye do, do it heartily, as to the Lord, and not unto men." Colossians 3:23

- I stand ready and always willing.
- I live to inspire myself.
- I am all in.
- I think highly of myself and what I am achieving.
- I am accountable for my success.
- I create a whirlwind of excitement.
- I am laser focused.
- I do my best work every day.
- I persevere to become an example for others.
- I finish what I start.

Fun Affirmation
I am my higher-self!

Courage Juice

Close your eyes. Imagine winning; imagine the goal won. Then, open your eyes, and review your game plan. This will supply you with the motivation and courage to move forward.

Proceed. Once in gear, advance into action towards your goal.

Find an accountability partner. This person does not have to be on the same journey as you. They are simply there for support.

Your Power Affirmations

Become your Higher-Self

OCCUPATION

Definition: Time you spend performing tasks as your source of livelihood.

"Six days thou shalt labour, and do all thy work."
Deuteronomy 5:13

- I am more than my job.
- I stand to reap the abundance of what I sow.
- I'm earning my way into a higher income bracket.
- I do great work out of self-respect.
- My wage and self-worth are two different things.
- I am upgrading my position and pay this year.
- I am an asset to any team.
- I am honest and above board.
- I am proud of my occupation.
- I am respected by my peers.

Fun Affirmation
I am surpassing my peers!

Mood Adjusters

Find pride. Use your job as a stepping stone. If you feel you have outgrown your position, you should plan, act, and proceed into the role aligned with your goals.

Realize. One of the biggest mistakes to happiness and peace is to place yourself behind money. Do not compromise your happiness for a paycheck.

Gratefulness. You can aspire to a new opportunity while grateful for the position you currently possess.

Your Power Affirmations

_____
_____
_____
_____
_____
_____
_____
_____
_____
_____
_____
_____
_____
_____
_____

Become your Higher-Self

PERFECTIONISM

Definition: Your refusal to accept a standard less than perfection.

"I have seen an end of all perfection."
Psalm 119:96

- God made me exactly how he wants me.
- I work quickly and efficiently.
- I take swift action towards the task at hand.
- I give my best, always.
- I am open to assistance from others.
- I am proud of all my work.
- I allow others to work at their pace.
- I like to see others find success in what they do.
- Life is more fun with a relaxed attitude.
- I am at peace with my work.

Fun Statement
I release it to the universe!

Mood Adjusters
Honor. Take pride in your work by keeping the end goal in mind while remaining relaxed and focused in order to do your best.

Realize. Technical situations need perfection. While most creative situations do not. Keeping this in mind will help you in determining when the job is done, when to move on, or to keep working at it.

Your Power Affirmations

Become your Higher-Self

REGRET

Definition: A sadness or disappointment you feel over a loss of something or an action against someone.

> *"If we confess our sins, He is faithful and just to forgive us of our sins..." 1 John 1:9*

- Today I live blessed.
- There are more opportunities coming my way.
- I have changed for the better.
- I am glad I have learned a lesson.
- Forgiveness is all I can ask for.
- Moving forward, I will do right by others.
- I am living in celebration.
- I am actively making corrections with others.
- I am in constant growth and change.
- I am courageous in all things.

Fun Statement
I dance with the skeletons in my closet!

Courage Juice
Write down 3 remedies to a mistake that is *eating* at you. Then jot down what their hopeful outcomes could be. Then, choose one remedy and move forward.

Face the ridicule. You can never outrun the feeling of regret, so you may as well turn around and face the embarrassment of your actions, and make peace with yourself. Only then can you begin to heal.

Forgive yourself. Life is not perfect for anyone – ever. So, relax.

Your Power Affirmations

Become your Higher-Self

SCHOOL

Definition: An institution where you receive education and instruction.

"But be thou an example of the believers, in word, in conversation, in charity, in spirit..." 1 Timothy 4:12

- I love applying what I learn.
- I do my best work always.
- I can grasp any subject.
- I respect my classmates and instructors.
- I will earn my degree(s) as planned.
- I make the most out of my experience.
- I am grateful for the teachers that guide me.
- Where I am headed is worth the work.
- I respect the rules as they keep me safe.
- I am determined to finish what I started.

Fun Affirmation
My path is clear!

Action Steps

Dedicate a schedule. Create a plan that includes time for school, friends, family and quality time alone.

Procrastination kills progress. Give your studies priority.

Rest. Your body and mind must rejuvenate in order for you to give your peak performance.

Network: School is a breeding ground for collaborations.

Your Power Affirmations

_____

_____

_____

_____

_____

_____

_____

_____

_____

_____

_____

_____

_____

_____

_____

_____

Become your Higher-Self

SELF-ESTEEM

Definition: Your confidence and satisfaction in yourself.

"Have I not commanded thee? Be strong and of a good courage; be not afraid..." Joshua 1:9

- I am worthy.
- I am a winner.
- I have everything I need to succeed.
- I am proud of who I am becoming.
- I deserve love and respect from others.
- My attire speaks confidence and pride.
- My opinion matters.
- I trust in me.
- I am capable of all things.
- I respect myself.

Fun Affirmation
I see greatness in my reflection!

Action Steps

Dress your best at all times. Even in your pajamas. When you see your reflection, you will be reminded of how amazing you are. Instant gratification.

Succeed in something today. Whether it is cleaning a room, reading a book or walking the dog. Completing a task is instant gratification and will boost your self-esteem.

See sections on <u>Confidence</u>, <u>Gratitude</u>, <u>Jealousy</u>, and <u>Self-Improvement</u>.

Your Power Affirmations

_____

_____

_____

_____

_____

_____

_____

_____

_____

_____

_____

_____

_____

_____

_____

Become your Higher-Self

SELF-IMPROVEMENT

Definition: Upping your status, education and so forth from your own personal efforts.

"For with God nothing shall be impossible."
Luke 1:37

- I woke up improved.
- I create my own opportunities to grow.
- I associate with great people.
- I read to develop my mind.
- I invest in myself and my future.
- I make the best decisions for my life, starting now.
- I choose water over sugary drinks.
- I exercise my body daily.
- I flaunt my talents.
- I grow stronger emotionally by the minute.

Fun Affirmation
I am super-superlative!

Action Steps

Itemize. List the changes you want to see in yourself. Choose a challenging transformation from that list, then give yourself a 90-day period to build that new habit.

Study media. Research self-improvement material that will help you grow into the person you have envisioned.

Do. Moving forward, perform at your best in all things. Even down to brushing your teeth and washing your face. Being at your best in the small things helps you to be at your best when facing the bigger challenges.

Your Power Affirmations

_____
_____
_____
_____
_____
_____
_____
_____
_____
_____
_____
_____
_____
_____
_____
_____

Become your Higher-Self

SICKNESS IN OTHERS

Definition: An illness, disease or indisposition effecting your loved one's mental or physical state.

"He giveth power to the faint." Isaiah 40:29

For you...
- I will help him/her be strong.
- I have courage.
- I will contribute where I have control.
- I accept God's plan.
- I am present.
- I am supportive.

For them...
- I am thankful for you in my life.
- We face this challenge together.
- You fight with strength and courage.
- You live your life celebrating.
- God gave you challenges to show strength to others.

Empowering Affirmation
We are warriors!

Courage Juice

Stay busy. Jump into an activity. This will help eliminate the gloom and helplessness you are feeling.

Help your loved one. Help them focus on the things they can control in spite of their disposition, and help them find the small successes to keep their spirits high.

Believe in your prayers. Your questions to and of God can only be answered if you truly believe. Otherwise, it is just a conversation you are having with yourself.

Your Power Affirmations

_____

_____

_____

_____

_____

_____

_____

_____

_____

_____

_____

_____

_____

_____

_____

Become your Higher-Self

SICKNESS IN YOU

Definition: An illness, disease or indisposition effecting your mental or physical state.

"For our light affliction..., worketh for us a far more exceeding and eternal weight of glory."
2 Corinthians 4:17

- I am strong in all things today.
- I live out my dreams, regardless.
- God gave me challenges to show strength to others.
- I accept guidance and support.
- I am grateful for those around me.
- I have dignity and grace in all situations.
- I accept challenges within my control.
- I fight with strength and courage.
- I live life celebrating.
- My dreams are alive and well.

Empowering Affirmation
I am a fighter!

Courage Juice
Focus on the things you can control in spite of your illness, and find the small successes to keep your spirits high.

If it is a long lasting affliction, find a support group who can relate. It is important to understand that friends and family may do their best, but may not know exactly how to help you.

See section on <u>Gratitude</u>.

Your Power Affirmations

Become your Higher-Self

STRESS

Definition: A state of mental or emotional strain from adversity or demanding situations.

"Let not your heart be troubled: ye believe in God, believe also in Me." John 14:1

- God gives me what I can handle.
- I am at my best under pressure.
- Challenges are strengthening tools for my character.
- Pressure is an opportunity to grow.
- I am equipped for anything coming my way.
- I am bigger than this situation.
- This circumstance is changeable.
- I am cool, and I am calm…*woosahhh. (Repeat)*
- I can handle whatever the outcome.
- I can see the end game and it's positive.

Fun Statement
Yes, yes, yes, and yes!

Mood Adjusters

Relocate momentarily or change your physical position to help ease pent-up tension.

Calisthenics. While taking long and deep breaths, perform light exercises such as stretching or walking.

Eat that ugly frog. Some stress is due to procrastination; dive in and work on what you are avoiding.

Leisure activity. Sometimes you just need a break. Read, watch a program, listen to music, etcetera.

Your Power Affirmations

_____
_____
_____
_____
_____
_____
_____
_____
_____
_____
_____
_____
_____
_____
_____
_____

Become your Higher-Self

TIME

Definition: Unending progression of being from the past, present and the future.

"So teach us to number our days, that we may apply our hearts unto wisdom." Psalm 90:12

- Greatness requires time and patience.
- I am grateful for this moment I am alive.
- I have an abundance of time to do what I desire.
- I work every minute of the day towards happiness.
- I live fulfilled and joyful.
- Patience is the key to all things that will be mine.
- My life is too big a gift to leave wrapped.
- I respect myself and other people's time.
- I enjoy the time I get to spend with loved ones.
- I am always on time.

Fun Affirmation
I do what I want – when I want!

Courage Juice
Whatever you have procrastinated on starting, put it on your calendar and commit to begin working on it.

Realize you will always have more to do than time will allow. Enjoy the process and do not spend your life rushing through things.

Love in the now. Loving after loss is always too late.

Live in the now. Living in the past or the future stops you from enjoying the life you are experiencing now.

Your Power Affirmations

Become your Higher-Self

UNDERSTANDING

Definition: When you are aware of other people's feelings; tolerant, forgiving and empathetic.

"He that hath knowledge spareth his words: and a man of understanding is of an excellent spirit."
Proverbs 17:27

- I am led by love.
- Only God should judge.
- I am a great listener.
- I am worthy of empathy from others.
- I am worthy of love.
- I surround myself with insightful people.
- I am kind to others in their time of need.
- I surround myself with those who strengthen me.
- I am empathetic towards my loved ones.
- I trust myself and the process of achieving my goals.

Fun Affirmation
I trust my journey!

Mood Adjusters

Write in your journal. Pour all of your concerns into it, for your journal will not judge you and it knows you the best.

Talk to someone who has been a great listener in the past. Only trust a few with your deepest troubles; those who will listen without judgment.

Allow someone to confide in you without you having all the answers. Most times, people are simply looking for a *shoulder* and compassion.

Your Power Affirmations

_____

_____

_____

_____

_____

_____

_____

_____

_____

_____

_____

_____

_____

_____

Become your Higher-Self

WINNING

Definition: When victory is yours!

"And He said. The things which are impossible with men are possible with God." Luke 18:27

- I will bask in my success.
- I win by remaining laser focused on my goals.
- I am fully committed to this purpose.
- I am a winner regardless of the outside outcome.
- Everything I do propels me towards my *win*.
- I possess a winner's spirit.
- Success is mine.
- I win because I do my best – always.
- I'm here. I see. I will conquer.
- I am at peace with my efforts.

Fun Affirmation
I can and I will!

Courage Juice

Reflect on a time when you have won in your life. That feeling will give you the courage you need now to move forward.

Posture up! Stand tall or sit up straight. This posture produces testosterone, which helps when facing a challenge.

Reward yourself. Treat yourself to something special when there is a job well done, even in the little wins.

Stay Ready. Remain in your highest form to face the challenges ahead. This gives you the upper hand.

Your Power Affirmations

_____

_____

_____

_____

_____

_____

_____

_____

_____

_____

_____

_____

_____

_____

Become your Higher-Self

YOU

Only you can define who you are.

"Therefore if any man be in Christ, he is a new creature." 2 Corinthians 5:17

You are the only one like **you.**

You can do all things you put into **action.**

You are a story **worthy** of sharing.

You are **unique** therefore special.

You share your gifts with the world.

You are **awake** and present.

You can change your life at any time you **choose.**

You have **permission** to live an amazing life.

You can **change** the world.

I **believe** in **you.**

Fun Fact
You are Awesomesauce!

I appreciate you. – *W. M. Jacey*

POWER AFFIRMATIONS FOR YOUR
HIGHER-SELF

Become your Higher-Self

*This book is dedicated to Carlotta and Jaime.
Thank you for working with me every single day, from
the beginning to the end of this project. Thank you for
being my support system, my cheerleaders and my
inspiration to complete this work.*

I love you to the end of days.

Thank you for investing in yourself with *On a Power Trip, Affirmations and Actions Towards Your Higher-Self.* We hope you continue to find value within these pages. Join the mailing list on www.wmjacey.com to be notified for upcoming book titles by, W. M. Jacey.

For <u>signed copies</u> of Ona a Power Trip, Affirmations and Actions Towards Your Higher-Self:

Order from www.wmjacey.com

Future Publications:

On A Power Trip, Affirmations and Actions For Entrepreneurs

On A Power Trip, Affirmations and Actions For Starting Over

Contact Information:

W. M. Jacey
www.wmjacey.com
Email: wmjacey@wmjacey.com
Mail: P.O. Box 2463
Riverside, CA 92516

Wrote Goat Publishing
P.O. Box 2463
Riverside, CA 92516
Email: letschat@wrotegoat.com